Decorative Beading

BETH BULLUSS

Decorative Beading

BETH BULLUSS

SALLYMILNER
PUBLISHING

First published in 2003 by
Sally Milner Publishing Pty Ltd
PO Box 2104
Bowral NSW 2576
AUSTRALIA

Design: Anna Warren, Warren Ventures
Diagrams: Anna Warren, Warren Ventures
Editing: Sylvia Kalan
Photography: Tim Connolly

Printed in China

National Library of Australia Cataloguing-in-Publication data

Bulluss, Beth.
 Decorative beading : lampshades, tassels, scarves, brooches
 and more delightful projects to make.

 ISBN 1 86351 319 1.

 1. Beadwork. I. Title. (Series : Milner craft series).

 745.582

Disclaimer
The information in this instruction book is presented in good faith. However, no warranty is
given, nor results guaranteed, nor is freedom from any patent to be inferred. Since we have no
control over the use of the information contained in this book, the publisher and the author
disclaim liability for untoward results.

10 9 8 7 6 5 4 3 2 1

For Rosaleen

"All the world's a stage..."
WILLIAM SHAKESPEARE

The Peta Lamp

Lavender dupion silk on a square shade with corner tilt is fringed with aqua, amethyst and silver beads. The resin base has a painted silver finish.

The Lee Lamp

Soft olive silk covers the scalloped Tiffany shade and it is trimmed with olive and taupe crystals, highlighted with large dress beads and small olive dress beads. Gold bugles and seed beads act as filler beads. The gold bugles give a gentle daylight face while the black seeds act as separator beads.

Contents

Introduction

ELCOME TO THE WORLD OF BEADED FRINGES. We have all observed the resurgence of beading as a means of ornamentation. In recent years, it has made its debut on the catwalk and as is always the case, once it has been featured on garments, the trend to use similar decorations in the home soon follows. Cushion and throw trims, key tassels, curtains and chair tie-backs, blind pulls, hair combs, brooches and picture frames are just a few of the current uses for beading.

As a glamorous touch, very little surpasses beading. We have only to look at the gowns chosen by Royalty, film stars and brides to know that special occasion gowns are enriched by the addition of beads.

The fringed necklaces that are so elegantly worn by both young and old are reminiscent of the wonderful decorations that adorned garments and furnishings of the 1920s.

Classes in jewellery-making are available for people of all ages. It is here that great creativity flourishes as the student is able to craft pieces to suit individual tastes and to produce unique and stunning accessories.

Beading classes across Australia are embroidering with beads both on garments and tapestries. Children and adults are flocking to classes to make Christmas decorations that are destined to become family heirlooms. The jug covers, so necessary for hygiene in the past, are now being treasured and copied for use in outdoor dining situations. Generous-sized

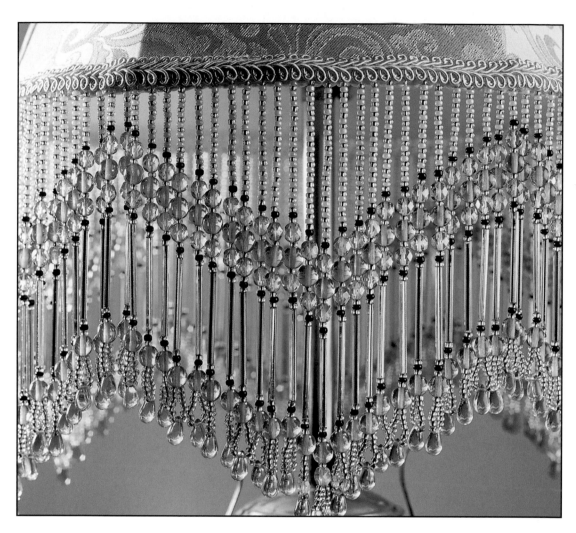

Detail of the Barbara Lampshade

salad bowls along with other food covers are being decorated and weighed down with enchanting beaded borders. Charming saris are further embellished with beaded tassels and then used as cloths for the barbecue and picnic tables.

Beading in all of its forms is a very relaxing and time-consuming hobby. Whether knitting, crocheting, embroidering, weaving or threading beads the same tactile and visual pleasure is felt. At the end of any project, in this truly aesthetic craft, there is always something new to delight the senses.

Lampshades decorated with beaded fringing are simply in a class of their own. Once you own one of these beautiful items, no others will measure against it. They create a bright spot in a dark corner in normal daylight and when lit, they have an ambience of warmth and style. Fringed lamps can blend in with décor of soft subtle tones or make an impact of bright colour. They can enhance the mood according to the availability of light. Different-coloured globes can also create different effects on the beads and the silk shades. These lamps are easily adapted in both traditional and modern decorating schemes.

The Barbara Lampshade

This straight-edged empire shade is covered in peach and gold brocade. Taupe, peach, cream and gold beads are used to form its opulent fringe. This shade has a beautiful daylight face as the gold threads reflect the light. Then, when lit, the brocaded pattern forms an elegant tracery above the beads.

The patterns should be first sketched onto graph paper for colour and general design placement and then physically threaded to check how they will hang. It can also be determined if they match or contrast with the shade covering.

A multitude of bases can be found in specialist shops and many Australian companies are willing to add extension to the candle of the base if requested. Antique bases are also readily available and are particularly suitable for traditional décor. Plant stands and ornaments can be electrified for unique bases.

The craft of beading a fringe for a lampshade is one of which you will never tire, in fact, you will find it strangely addictive. The results of your labours will be a treasured possession that is not only useful but it is also decorative. All you need to have is patience and persistence.

This book is project rich. The small projects can be completed fairly quickly and the advantages of attempting them are many:

❖ Providing experience in the handling of the beads

❖ An opportunity for experimentation with colour, pattern and bead types

❖ The finished product is a lovely keepsake or handmade gift for use or sale.

Why Bead?

ALMOST EVERY ARTICLE RELATING TO HEALTH tells us that people are increasingly sedentary. This is true, but many are sedentary for periods of their lives due to circumstances beyond their control. Some are aged, others injured or recovering from injury —others still are recuperating from surgery or personal trauma. People too, have blocks of 'free' time, when they choose to follow less active pursuits.

Beading is a craft that can be pursued by anyone wishing to make a beautiful object using their hands, their senses and concentrating their mind on pleasurable activity. Then, on the completion of the project, their satisfaction is increased with the practically of a delightful item.

This method of beading is an activity that can be easily picked up and put down and as the patterns are concise, it is quick to comprehend.

Not only is it aesthetically pleasing, the play of light on the beads, the cool kindliness of the glass to the touch, the teasingly appealing development and growth of the pattern and the pure colour pleasure all contribute to feelings of calm delight. Gasps of pleasure are the most common sounds to be heard in a beading class.

This very therapeutic craft revives one of the gentle arts. Beading is calming. Many rushed or agitated students have, within a period of ten minutes, settled and centred themselves to become increasingly absorbed in their work. The simple

This ceiling shade is a scalloped Tiffany which has been covered in white dupion silk. The fringe is in colours to compliment other lamps in the general area. A diffuser globe works well to give directional lighting over a dining table.

pleasure gained from concentrating and working towards a goal using tactile materials soothes the most troubled soul. There is also a strong sense of community spirit amongst these like-minded people as they give positive feedback and exchange ideas and materials.

As previously stated, beading is addictive! Evidence of this diversity is depicted by the large number of projects created for this book. Even the most dedicated of quilters, who also consider themselves to be beaders, may be persuaded to leave their quilts for long periods of time. Sometimes they prefer the convenience of having all their materials on a smaller working area than that to which they are accustomed. The extra light and life of beads has further enhanced their use of colours and their preparedness to take colour risks. Of course, they have also brought knowledge of what works for them in their craft and benefit from the exchange of ideas that apply to all areas of colour and design. Many combine the two crafts in their crazy patchwork projects. Folk artists are using beading to add another dimension to their craft too, and there are examples of this in the tassel tops and brooch projects contained in this book.

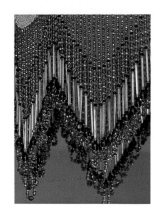

The many small projects in this book will be useful to try when beading for the first time. Most can be accomplished very quickly. A lampshade, however, needs serious commitment of interest, time and money. However, all of the beaded fringes demonstrated within these pages so versatile that they can be adapted or modified to suit any of the other projects shown. Last, but not by any means least, this method of beading is very easy and so, creative energies are free to come into force and produce some remarkably beautiful objects.

Getting Started

THE PROJECTS IN THIS BOOK HAVE BEEN designed for first-time beaders as well as for those who wish for further challenges in this exciting craft.

If you are coming to the craft of beading for the first time, the following photograph will help with bead identification.

Of course, bead descriptions will vary amongst suppliers, but an attempt has been made to reach a consensus to assist in the search for the beads of your choice. Many suppliers have catalogues for sale. This is a small investment if you are ordering by mail.

The range of beads used in the photographs within this book include:

❖ seed beads or rocailles

❖ pearls

❖ small and large dress (otherwise known as smooth pressed glass beads or Tiffany beads)

❖ bugle beads

❖ tubes (oversized bugle beads)

❖ cut beads (often referred to as crystals)

Others may be feature beads such as daggers, leaves, hearts, frogs, birds, insects, shells and man-made clay shapes with holes in them.

Be careful as some of the beads have rough interior holes that will damage your thread. Imitation pearls are just glass beads covered with a film. This film can cause your thread to fray. If you are using pearls, stab a pin through this layer on both sides of the bead to help reduce the wear and tear on the thread.

Many beads are dyed or painted. Colourfast beads are better suited for lamps. Before applying any beads, first test for

Samples of beads

Clockwise from bottom left: texture drops, bugle beads, seed beads, small dress beads, large dress beads, cut beads, fancy beads and centre, tubes.

colour permanence by soaking with a 1:1 part solution of bleach and water. Alternatively, you can leave a few beads overnight in acetone (nail varnish remover).

A warning about bugle beads — these are simply tubes of glass and often have very sharp edges. The edges can be gently filed smooth using an emery board. It is also wise to feel each end of a bugle bead prior to threading it onto the cotton.

There is, of course, a large range in sizes. For the purpose of the dangle method of construction, the bead shaft must allow the needle and four thicknesses of the chosen thread to pass through. It is very frustrating indeed to have threaded down the bead and then to find that it is impossible to get the needle through the beads on the return journey up to the tape! The exception is when you wish to use a very small seed bead. This can be used in the loop part at the bottom of the strand, where the thread is two thicknesses on each side of the loop. The range of beads produced by Delica are very pretty in the loop sections.

Beads are numbered according to size The lower the bead number, the smaller the bead. As the bead sizes decrease, so too does the hole size. For projects in this book, with the exception of limited use of Delica seed beads, seed beads size nine or larger have been used.

Some Delica beads have been used in the loop section at the bottom of the strands for colour impact. (Refer to diagram below showing the passage of the thread through the loop.)

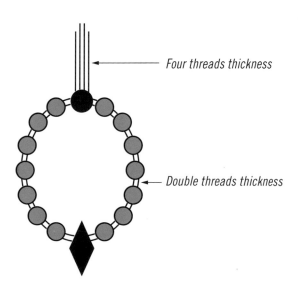

Four threads thickness

Double threads thickness

NEEDLES

CrownFox needles in size No.2C are very satisfactory for beading fringes. These are fine needles with a good-sized eye and are slightly flexible. Many of the quality quilting needles are simply too fine for the cotton and are often too rigid. Having a needle that is easy to thread removes the temptation to use a thread that is too long to manage. Excessively long threads will wear with the constant pulling through the beads, especially where several bugle beads or pearls are used in each strand. An added bonus with a No.2C CrownFox needle is that the short leftover tails of the cotton can be re-threaded and used. Thread one strand of cotton, then the next piece above it, through the generous eye of this needle. Much waste can be prevented using this simple technique.

Note Broken needles are dangerous! If you break a needle, tape the pieces to paper and fold it over. Then, keep the paper in a labelled screw top jar for disposal.

THREAD

Nymo is the beading thread of choice for many experienced beaders. It is a polyester thread that is slightly waxed. This thread is particularly easy to thread but if undoing is required, the thread often separates and becomes frayed. Nymo is available in a wide range of colours and can be stored on a spool or a cone.

Coates' polyester-coated cotton quilting thread is another suitable thread to use. It also comes in a wide variety of colours. The weight of this thread is preferable and you can use white, cream or black for most of your work. Dark-coloured threads will produce a shadow within the bead while light-coloured threads do not affect the colour to any great degree. Coloured threads can be used to enhance or intensify the colour of a bead particularly a transparent glass bead.

Many commercially purchased beaded fringes have very long, clear glass bugle beads. These are generally threaded on white cotton, which gives the beads the appearance of being disconnected with the rest of the pattern. A coloured thread in this situation would unite the whole design.

LIGHTING

Natural light is perfect. A dual halogen light is suitable, however the lower intensity is satisfactory for all but the work with very tiny beads. It is handy to switch to more power if you need to do so. At night, eyestrain can be avoided by combining task light with low-level incandescent background lighting. Ideally you should position your light so that the work is illuminated from above and from the side. Be sure that the light you use gives you true colour — that is, colour as close as possible to that viewed in strong natural light.

TIPS FOR BEGINNERS

❖ Using a plate or tray with an edge along with a white table napkin is an excellent work surface. This will keep the beads contained and give good light reflection. Many beaders have trays that have been covered with fine leather and they work very well. The removable lid from an unlined sewing box could be lined with leather and a working surface would always be available.

❖ Mark tape spacing with a soft pencil or in the case of dark tape use a silver or gold fine-point pen.

❖ Use shorter rather than longer threads.

❖ Save end threads of cotton for short rows.

❖ Always finish off a strand of beading and move the needle and thread to the next dot on the tape before putting work away for the day. Often, failure to do this results in resuming the beading at the already completed strand and then it has to be undone.

❖ Cotton or silk bias folded strips are more desirable than loosely woven cotton tape. If the beading has to be undone, it is easier to pull the threads through the silk without damage. There is no stretching problem as there is stitching at every strand that holds the bias fabric quite firm. Folded cotton bias binding also works well.

- ❖ The silk, folded bias strips, made from the same coloured silk (or other shade fabric), are inconspicuous when applied to the shade. If the final covering braid has a very open texture, it will still cover the 'workings' on the silk folded tape.

- ❖ Spend more rather than less time on pattern development.

- ❖ For the best effect, view several strands of the pattern in the shade and in all other types of light.

- ❖ If in doubt, pull it out.

- ❖ Work in short sessions as a tired neck and eyes affect concentration and contribute to the making of mistakes.

- ❖ Vary your work place. It is lovely to work in natural light on a deck, veranda or in the garden. Good quality light makes for easy work.

- ❖ Look at nature for the best colour combinations. Even a single flower has many shades of colour and many different values of colour. These colours transfer wonderfully to bead designs.

- ❖ Purchase all bead supplies for one project at the same time. This will ensure that all of the beads come from the same colour batch. There are many uses for small quantities of left over beads.

- ❖ If your thread twists, hold up your fringing and let the needle hang down. The thread will slowly untwist.

- ❖ When starting a strand, knot the thread and sew into the tape. Make sure the knot is mid-way in the tape. Then sew a small neat stitch on the edge at the marking dot. Knots on the edge are difficult to sew through and make the edge pucker. Tugging the needle through a secured knot can also cause the eye of the needle to snap.

- ❖ If you discover you have a few too many seed beads on your strand, they can be cut out using pliers. Do not attempt to cut out large beads or bugles as the cut glass pieces will slice the thread. Safety is important here as well. Hold the bead well away from your eyes so that the bits don't fly and cause damage.

FRAMES

Modern lampshade frames are wire-based and then plastic-coated. This eliminates rust problems. If you are recycling a frame, strip it down, sand it and then paint it with white gloss paint. Check that any reused frames have no bends or dings that will cause problems in covering or that will distort the shape of the shade.

Many shapes and sizes are available. Sizes are always provided in imperial measurements. Samples can be viewed at craft and decorating shops. Obviously, the shade shape should reflect the general decorating style of the room, not oppose it.

Frame classification varies slightly from one manufacturer to another. Generally, a sheet with numbered frames is available for ordering from craft and decorating stores.

For the purpose of beading a shade, simple shapes work best. A wide variety of shapes have been incorporated into this book to demonstrate the various uses of different shade styles.

Overall balance of the base and the fringe length is vital. Viewing it in situ is the best way to see if the visual balance is harmonious.

Most of the frame styles can be ordered in a range of sizes. An eight-inch frame is satisfactory as a feature, but the ten inch is the best of the small frames to show the beading to an advantage.

Using the same style of frame in a combination of sizes works well in the one general area. Beading patterns need not be identical, but the colours need to be harmonious with the décor.

If you are purchasing a pair of shades frames, make sure that you buy them at the same time and from the same supplier. There is some variation depending on the assembler. There is also wide variation within the same style. For example, in the Tiffany range of shades, some have a more steeply curved strut. These are a little harder to cover than the frames with a gentle strut curves. The examples in the photographs have been described with the most common name, but some liberty has been taken with some of the descriptions to help in frame choice.

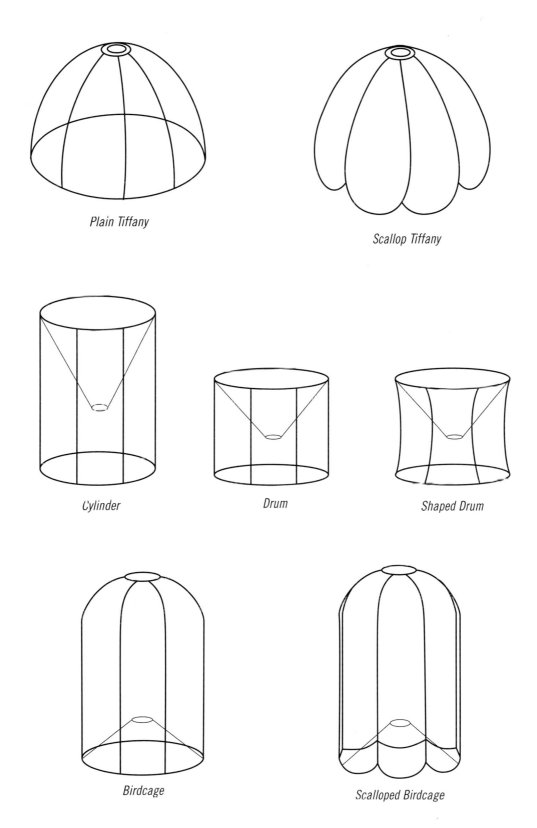

Plain Tiffany

Scallop Tiffany

Cylinder

Drum

Shaped Drum

Birdcage

Scalloped Birdcage

Diagrams of Frames

Diagram 1 – Shapes of lampshade frames

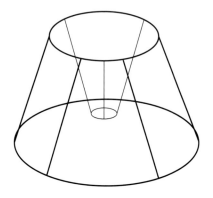

Straight Empire

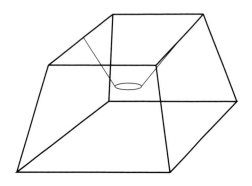

Square Empire

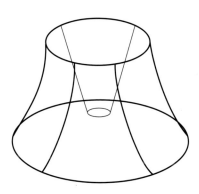

Shaped Empire

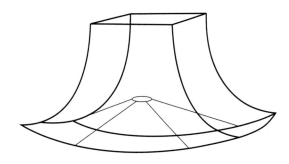

Pagoda

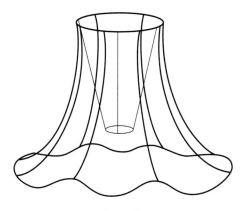

Domonique

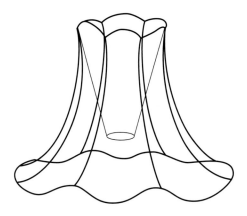

Scalloped Domonique

LININGS

Generally, linings need to be white or ivory for good light reflection and to hide the mechanics of the shade. If greater intensity of colour is required, the same tone as the outside covering could be used.

The lamps in this book have all been lined with nylon net fabric, cut on the bias and stretched for a taut finish. Flame retardant spray can be applied to the lining at this stage if so desired. Lace, used as a backing fabric to the outer covering, will give an interesting finish. The lace is barely obvious until the shade is lit and then the effect of the pattern is very charming. As an internal edge finish at the bottom of the shade, a row of white gimp (braid) will give a neat appearance.

SHADE COVERINGS

Fabrics suitable for shades are many and varied. Choose a fabric that can be ironed.

The bindings that are used to cover the joins in the shade need to be an ironed bias strip of the same fabric. Many polyester fabrics do not give a neat finish to the exterior shade. Some shades have gimp over the seam joins, but this can be too distracting. The main feature should be the beads, so avoid embellishing the seam covers with gimp. Seams covered in folded bias lamp fabric give an inconspicuous finish. Silk, taffeta, linen, cotton, brocade, shantung and combinations of these all work well. Plain fabrics, stripes, checks, floral and lace are just a few of the fabric finishes available for use.

BRAIDS

Whether you choose to work on narrow woven cotton tape or narrow folded bias strips in the same fabric as your shade, you will need a covering braid to finish off your shade. This can blend or contrast with the shade. It can also be a feature if further enhancement of the shade or bead colour is required.

Sometimes an edge is enhanced with a combination of braids. In this case, it would be desirable to use a wide and a narrow braid, rather than two of the same width. Braid in the same colour as the shade with either gold or silver trim is a possible combination.

The most commonly used braid is gimp which has a regular but fairly flexible weave. Rigid or very closely woven braids work well on shades that have a straight edge. The braids most commonly used on shades in this book are the basic braids (often referred to as gimp) and these are very easy to apply around scallops and other curved edges.

The length of braid needed to cover the waist of the tassel varies greatly according to the circumference of the waist of the tassel top. Whilst the amount is always relatively small, it is necessary to measure the waist of the tassel top and allow extra when cutting. Joins need to be as inconspicuous as possible and there is no difficulty in aligning the ends of the basic braid.

Try using the following method

❖ Measure the required amount to fit the edge and before cutting, allow an extra 1¼ in (3.1 cm).

❖ Run the glue over a length of approximately ¾ in (2 cm) at each end and allow it to dry. This will prevent fraying of the rayon threads.

The Joy Lamp

A converted garden ornament forms the base of this lamp. A double-scalloped Tiffany shade is covered in magnificent magenta/aqua taffeta and complemented with rich magenta and aqua beads.

❖ Cut one end between the loops on the braid or gimp on a slight angle. This gives two 'legs'.

❖ Cut the other end close to the curves but with no 'legs'.

❖ Dovetail these together for a perfect join.

More care is needed to match elaborate braids but there are some highly decorative examples available.

For a more elegant finish, a perfectly matching braid to the fabric is desirable. Here it is possible to dye your own braids to get the identical match.

TAPE

When beading, the tape is the anchor point for the threaded beads. The start of the strand is on the edge of the tape and the finish of the strand is in the same place on the edge after the needle is returned, via a loop, up the strand of beads.

Narrow cotton tape that is firmly woven or bias folded silk strips are both satisfactory for general use. Care must be taken to colour match the tape or folded bias strips if a loosely woven braid is used to cover the working tape at the end of the project.

The tape must always be slightly narrower than the decorative covering braid.

GLUE

Most craft glues are suitable for attaching the completed length of beaded fringing to the tassel tops, shelf edges, combs and lampshade edges. Glue should be applied to the braid, not to the edge of the project. Press firmly until the braid adheres and trim as required. On a free edge, such as a comb, shelf or lampshade, gentle pegging with clothes pegs will assist adhesion Do not leave the pegs on for too long a time as any excess glue will cause the pegs to adhere as well.

BASES

Many of the lovely tall slim bases in current vogue are perfect for a lamp with a beaded shade. The shade proportions are different when there is the extra length of 8 in (20 cm) in the

visual and actual length of a beaded shade. All styles of bases
can be modified by an electrician so that the candle section of
the base is longer than normal.

The availability of a wide range of bases includes plaster,
ceramic, brass, silver, iron, fibreglass or resin, favourite
ornaments or objects from nature. In fact the choice is open to
what ever suits your taste and décor.

Ideally, the base should be chosen before the shade frame.
The single, most important factor to be considered when
choosing a base is the distance from where the decorative part
of the lamp base ends to the point at which the drop-fitting
shade frame sits. This part is called the candle.

Many exquisite bases are now designed for the decorative
part to end with a cup, a tassel feature or a turned section.
Above this the unadorned candle extension is a smooth column
in a neutral colour such as cream. Though they are more

Benjamin Night Light

expensive to buy, these bases are ready for immediate use. Many lighting manufacturers are willing to modify your base at the point of production and this is more desirable for overall finish. It is also cheaper than having to have a new base modified.

If the base you have chosen needs to have a candle extension added, or the existing one extended, try the shade next to the lamp and measure the distance from the drop fitting base to where you want the candle to meet the lamp fitting. This measurement determines the size of the longest strand of beads in your beaded fringe.

It is important to have a well-balanced sturdy base as the beaded fringes become heavy. If you find a base that is visually

Diagram 2 –
Lamp Bases

Lamp base without extension   *Lamp base with extension*

perfect for your situation, but so light that it will be easily knocked over, there are solutions. The base can be weighted with a moulded piece of lead inserted into a turned out section at the base. Another method is to have an extra turned-timber base added. Often, an extra base section can assist in the overall visual balance and impact of the finished lamp. The cherub bases in this book have had turned wooden plinths added for visual balance.

Sometimes the stem of the base continues on to become the candle part and this works very well. An example of this would be a fully turned Jacobean timber stem or a wrought iron base with a continuous stem. Here, the look is tall and elegant. Manufacturers will extend the base to candle height at production.

Caitlin Night Light

The Pagoda Shade

The pagoda-shaped frame is covered with a deep-shade of purple silk. Amethyst, olive, black and gold beads make up the chevron pattern. The extra length and feature drops accentuate the corner tilt of the shade.

If you like the look of an object for a lamp base, it is worth your while spending some time working out how it can be adapted or modified. In this way you will have a unique base. The Benjamin Night Light on page 32 and the Caitlin Night Light on page 35 are examples of using favourite ornaments which have been converted into attractive lamps for a child's room. The bear was originally a little moneybox while the figurine has been attached to a small base.

COLOUR

As in any creative endeavour, colour is the key to success. Of course, personal preferences and the final location of your lamp

will play an important part in your colour selection, but the rules for using colours must still be observed for an harmonious outcome.

With glass beads, the play of external light in daylight hours as well as the impact of internal light when your lamp is lit must be taken into account. It is here that the smooth surface of the glass beads and the cut beads are particularly effective. A variety of seed beads in gold, silver or colours in the scheme can act as filler beads, but the smooth dress beads and crystals are definitely the focus beads.

The use of a dark bead, such as black, navy or a silver-lined amethyst will act as separator beads which will in turn,

make the other colours appear stronger and accentuate groupings of beads, forming a pattern line. White beads will do the same if used solely as separators within the pattern.

CHANDELIER OR WALL SCONCES

As lovely as chandeliers are, the glare produced by the globes can be made softer by the addition of very small shades.

Two 6 in (15 cm) straight empire shades have been covered with a paisley fabric. A short beaded fringe in coordinating colours has been added.

For beading purposes, table chandelier frames need to be made shorter than usual. Then, a dainty fringe that is in harmony with the surrounding crystals can be used as a trim. For the shade coverings, black, white and cream will always work well. Bright or jewel coloured shades could be used to echo other accessories in a room.

This table chandelier has a tiny pair of shade frames covered in a bright fuchsia silk fabric. The short fringe is made with silver seed beads, tiny crystals and a feature fuchsia crystal in the centre of each panel. It was important to use a subtle fringe that did not compete with the other crystals on the lamp.

The two shades above were worked as samples to show the use of various beads and fabrics. The lamp on the left is covered in cream silk, fringed in pearls with peach crystals and the lamp on the right is decorated with floral fabric complete with an amethyst and pink fringing.

Why Lamps?

OFTEN THE AFTERTHOUGHT IN DECORATING, lamps nevertheless will bring colour elements together, balance the visual effects in a room and provide ambience in a way that no other form of lighting is able to do.

Beaded lampshades cannot be easily compared to any other decorated lamp as they are one of a kind and this uniqueness gives them top place as decorative devices. Beaded shades lit in a room at night are inviting and set a lovely tone.

They have two distinct faces — the daylight and unlit face where the beads reflect any interplay of daylight, and the warm soft-lit face where bead and shade colours are heightened for glorious night-time effect.

Directional task lighting is, of necessity, quite strong, but this needs to be balanced with ambient lighting and whilst atmosphere can be created with candles, a safer and cleaner light would be provided by a beaded lampshade.

Shades with elegant fringes are useful and decorative as both standard and table lamps. When these are placed next to sofas or single chairs, they will supply mood lighting for the whole room and adequate task lighting for reading.

For a bedside table, ensure that the lamp is the correct height for reading in bed and use a low wattage pearl globe that will cast sufficient light.

A night light in an infant's room can be a small beaded shade. Placed high on a chest and with a low wattage globe, it would give a very soft and comforting light. Refer to the Caitlin and Benjamin Night Lights on pages 32 and 35.

Probably, the most important reason for the choice of lamps as an integral part of the room's décor is the flattering quality of light. Faces appear softer and furniture and fabrics take on a mellow tone.

Detail of Rose Silk Lamp

Rose Silk Lamp

An empire frame has been covered in pale pink silk. Peach and pink dyes merge to give a dramatic looking looped fringe. Over this olive, pink and peach beads form a regular pattern. Beautiful velvet roses add an opulent touch to this shade.

The Carol Lamp

This lamp is designed to enhance any period setting. The highly ornamental base rests on a mahogany wine table and together with the rich colours of the amethyst, pink, burgundy and gold, complements the antique furniture. The fringing is stunning yet simple.

Detail of the Carol Lamp

Salon Style Lamp

The pointed Tiffany shade is covered in white rose brocade. The fringing has delicate pink and white beads.

Detail of the Salon Style Lamp

Using
Antique Beads

SOURCING ANTIQUE BEADS CAN BE A REAL TREASURE hunt. Often, auction boxes contain a few strands of usable beads but every now and then a small section of damaged bead fringing reveals wonderful colour schemes and interesting patterns. Many fringed shades from the 1920s are simple two-colour patterns arranged in a delightful fall of beads. The chevron pattern was used effectively and black separating beads enhanced even the most simple pattern arrangements.

When buying second-hand beads, be aware that there is often wearing in the shaft. If this area has become very rough, it will act like sandpaper on your thread and the beading will not last. As well, it would be advisable to check the finish on the ends of any bugle beads. Many have a well-rounded and smooth finish, but some are excessively sharp and irregular and would be risky to thread. Of course, in some instances you could file the ends of the bugles on emery paper or use a glass grinder if there were some special beads that you wished to salvage.

Sometimes, beads that have been dyed or painted have lost most of their colour and even their lustre. View them for their shape and use them in conjunction with beads that would add to their appearance. For example, small new cut beads placed

The Ada Lamp

This inverted scallop Tiffany lampshade has mainly seed beads in pink, cream and gold. Black seed beads separate the colours and a tiny black crystal finishes the strand. The pomegranate pink damask highlights the paisley design when unlit

Detail of Ada Lamp

between two old glass beads that have an interesting shape would still produce a lovely effect. It is wise to clean old beads by soaking in a 1:1 part solution of bleach and water, then rinsing in hot water and leaving them to dry in the sun.

Beaded Lamps
Suit Every Décor

**A** COMMENT FREQUENTLY MADE IS THAT beaded lampshades only suit traditional décor. However, beaded lampshades will suit all decorating styles. These include country farmhouse, city sophisticate, beach house, art deco and contemporary living. Special occasion lamps can made for gold and silver anniversaries, Christmas and weddings. It is simply a matter of shade choice, colour suitability and bead pattern.

When compiling items for this book, the shade shapes, fabrics, beads, patterns and the bases, consideration was given to particular styles of furniture, furnishings and accessories usually located in a room. Feature lamps shown are those that have used unusual bases or favourite ornaments as part of the whole lamp arrangement. Also included are the lamps designed for a specific setting.

Other suggestions for feature lamps are:

❖ A driftwood and shell base with a sand or sea-coloured shade. The beads could be in sea tones with edges resembling white caps worked in pristine white beads in assorted sizes.

❖ A favourite trophy could be converted into a base and serve a more useful purpose.

The Peony Rose Lamp

This lamp is one of a pair featured in a casual living setting. The room has natural cane lounges with cream cotton seat cushions. The cushions and the lamps are covered in the same fabric. The beads chosen for the lamp fringe contain all of the colours in the room. The timber base echoes the cane colours and is not too formal for the setting.

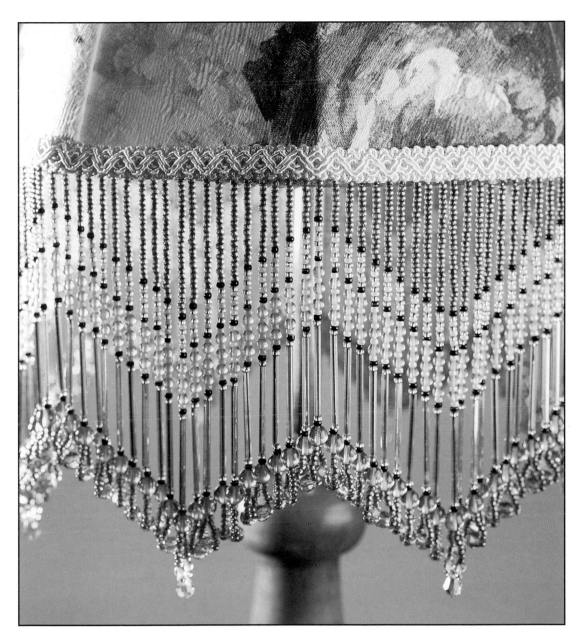

Detail of Peony Rose Lamp

❖ Bronzed baby shoes could be attached to the base and some vintage fabrics, christening gown skirt and/or laces could be used to cover a shade. A beaded fringe could be created with beads from family sewing boxes or its mother's wedding dress.

❖ Hopefully, the variety of styles in this book will assist in the choices available.

Care of Beaded Lampshades

**O**NCE YOU ARE THE PROUD OWNER OF ONE OF these treasures, you will want to care for it. Simply, the shade needs to be kept dust free. The shade and the beads can be cleaned with a hair drier. A fine brush, such as a baby's hairbrush can also be used. Brush the shade inside and out, then gently brush down the length of the beaded fringe on both sides.

If you wish to wash the whole shade, this can also be done. Firstly, remove the shade from the base. Use a product for washing woollens and simply dunk the whole shade in warm water containing a weak solution of wool wash. Gently rotate the shade in the water until it is clean. Gently rinse in warm water until all the detergent has been removed. Pat the shade and beads dry and then place the shade on a towel laying on a flat surface. As drying occurs, towel dry any wet areas and rotating the shade. Take care at all times that the beads hang as straight as possible. When finished, reassemble the shade to the base and enjoy the fresh sparkle of the clean beads.

Another important part of shade care is the need to use the correct globes to light the lamps. A low wattage globe will give the soft ambient light so necessary for shades and will also prevent overheating and fading. Be aware that many of the silk fabrics will fade with normal use, but this is not unattractive and will just be a subtle shading of the original colour.

The Margaret Lamp

This little Tiffany lamp has a straight edge. The shade colour has been matched to the verdigris finish on the cherub base. Designed for a shelf in a clients' conservatory the lamp has a traditional feel that looks wonderful amongst the surrounding foliages in the conservatory.

Detail of the Margaret lamp

Using Beaded Fringes on Standard Lamps

SHADES WITH BEADED FRINGES CAN ALSO BE USED on standard lamps. The Grace Lamp is a fine example. Frames for standard lamps need to be at least 16–18 in (40–45 cm) so that the proportions are harmonious. The fringing is very heavy so it is wise to do it in four sections for ease of application to the shade edge. Stitching and gluing will give added adhesion. Many small beads can be combined with striking features bead such as large crystals for a good visual effect. Generally, however, a larger bead such as a ⅛ in (3 mm) dress or crystal would be easier to use than masses of small seed beads for such a large project.

The Grace Lamp

Here the very long amber tubes have been combined with topaz, gold, amber and
black beads. The overall length of the shade, including fringing, is 36 in (90 cm) so
it is suitable for a standard lamp.

The Dangle Method of Construction

 LL OF THE PROJECTS IN THIS BOOK HAVE BEEN assembled using the dangle method of construction. Simply, this is attaching a double thread to a bias tape, threading the beads onto the thread, forming a loop at the end of the strand (to facilitate the turn) and then returning the thread back through all the remaining beads. Finally, the thread is secured into the tape with a holding stitch. The next strand is attached at the required space from the last and the process repeats.

The space between the threads is dependent on many factors. Too much space could affect the unity of the design or interfere with the visual requirements of the pattern. For example, a butterfly, flower or initial would need the bead strands placed very closely together to achieve blocks of colour and good pattern reproduction. If the spacing is too far apart, the pattern elongates and distortion occurs.

A chevron pattern needs approximately ¼ in (6 mm) spacing or more depending on the width of the widest bead. If a large feature bead has been chosen, care must be taken not to place the strands too closely together. The pattern may not hang true and will need to be corrected using wider spacing. However, there is some appeal and extra light reflection for beads that hang one strand forward and one strand back. This can happen if the feature beads have a greater diameter than the spacing between the strands.

The shape of the scallop or edge can also affect spacing of the beads. A deep-scalloped shade may need fewer beads in between the scallops to avoid crowding. A sharp-angled peak on a shade edge may need the beads further apart to facilitate an attractive fall of the beads.

There are many other kinds of bead application and ornamentation — bead weaving, bead knitting, bead crochet and French bead embroidery. These could all be used as trims in conjunction with the dangle method of construction.

In the dangle method of construction, the pattern can be worked out on graph paper or tried on cotton thread. The increases and decreases along a grid on the graph paper create the ups and downs in the finished strand. One long strand in the centre of a pattern gives a point, whereas several long strands in the centre can produce a rounded finish. A simple pattern of one long strand of beads alternating with one short strand of beads is also very effective.

Pattern Design

THE BUSINESS OF PATTERNING BEADS FOR A
design is as varied as the patterns that you
can produce. If you are trying beaded fringes
for the first time you may find this method useful:

1   Choose two of your favourite colours, for example, blue and
green.

2   Make a vertical pattern using the coloured pencils on ⅛ in
(3 mm) grid graph paper. You may do three blue, one
green, three blue, etc. It is referred to as strand 1 in
diagram 3.

3   Now observe which colour predominates in your design. Is
it the blue or the green? The one that is in greater amount
either in quantity or intensity becomes your feature, and the
finished pattern will be mainly that colour and your colour
of preference over the other colour. You may reverse the
colours at this stage as you play with the general appearance
of the two colours together.

4   Now, redo the colour pattern adding a black square to break
up some parts of the pattern. You may now have three
blue/one black/one green/three blue/one green/one black.
Repeat this much once more, down the vertical pattern. You
will observe that the black bead acts as a separator bead and
accentuates the other colours. For the purpose of pattern

development, the beads that lie between the black beads represent a section. Referred to this diagram as strand 2.

5   For the next strand, on either side of the black, colour-in a silver or gold square. This adds a bit of sparkle and extra light reflection to the beads.

6   Redo the pattern, however this time, block in seven squares in gold, in the place of one of the gold squares. This represents a one-inch bugle bead and adds a whole new area for the play of light. Referred to this diagram as strand 3.

7   All the squares have equal visual weight, so now is the time to try out the design with beads of different lengths and widths. You will need to do this with a needle and thread. So, keeping to the colours you have chosen, but changing the sizes of the sections with different beads, you will now have a really clear idea of what your pattern will look like. Use the last gold bead of your pattern as a junction bead. Add an extra thirteen blue seed beads for your loop and then transfer your pattern to thread and tape. Referred to this diagram as strand 4.

8   Complete three identical strands and then view them in both day and night light next to the fabric of you choice.

9   Keep experimenting until you are really satisfied with your colour and bead combinations.

10 Have a look — do you want a gold seed bead between the blue and green beads? Try it. Perhaps you want the beads above and below the bugle bead to be the same. By experimenting, you will find what is aesthetically pleasing.

11 An excellent idea at this time is to make up a tassel in your design. It can always be a gift and will certainly give you a good idea of the success of your design.

Diagram 3 – Pattern Design

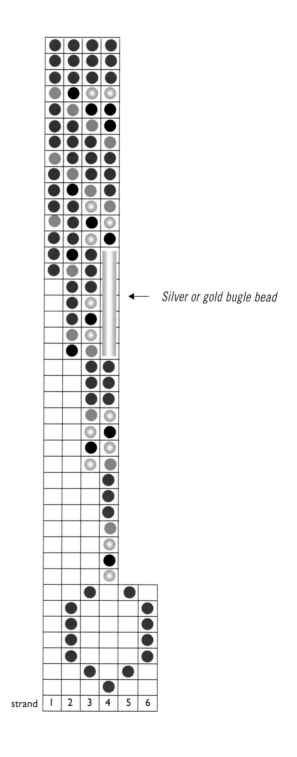

← Silver or gold bugle bead

strand	1	2	3	4	5	6

Pattern Development

THE INCREASES AND DECREASES THAT GIVE THE chevron pattern to the beaded fringes can be located anywhere within in the length of the fringing strands.

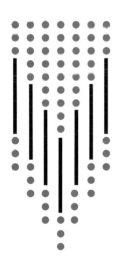

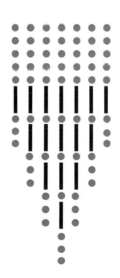

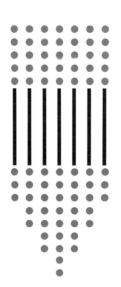

Diagram 4 – Pattern Development

Personal preference will dictate choice.

Figure 1 – the pattern increases and decreases are in the top section.

Figure 2 – has used short bugle beads for increases and decreases in the centre section.

Figure 3 – increases and decreases for the chevron are at the bottom section.

The Judith Tassels – Small and Large

A selection of tassels with decorated tops, multi-dyed rayon underskirts and beaded overskirts.

Tassels

W HEN THE VARIOUS TASSELS FOR *BEADED Lampshades* were designed, the intention was to devise projects that could be made reasonably quickly that would teach the handling of the fine needle and beads. As well, they would provide an opportunity to identify the various kinds of beads used in the dangle method of construction.

From the original tassel project, tassels of different degrees of fullness and sizes have been made to produce decorative devices for a wide range of interior uses. Some of these include key tassels, blind cord pulls, curtain tie-backs, features for the centre of pelmets, tablecloth weights and for the ends of table runners, parcel ornaments, brooches, scarves, neck tassels and glorious Christmas decorations. The bead and cord sizes are varied to suit the particular project. These will all be cherished gifts.

There are many projects that use a very small amount of beaded fringes effectively. These small sections of fringing can be applied to and combined with other hand-crafted items to make something that is unique. Sources of inspiration could be old movies ('Casablanca' has many beaded shades in the café), old necklaces (these can be found in charity shops), old silk fringes and the colours in nature. History of costume books contain inspiring for ideas for lampshades.

Making the Lyndel Tassel

The basic tassel, The Lyndel Tassel, has proven itself to be a winner. After completing one, the steps to variation are simple. Colours, bead and cord sizes, number and length of strands and the patterns can be changed. Then added variety can be achieved by using different tassel tops. As with all of the straight tassels, only one strand of pattern is shown. The pattern is then simply repeated for the required number of strands.

The Lyndel Tassel Stages

Clockwise, from top centre: One completed strand, twelve completed strands, three tassels showing colour alternatives to the basic pattern, two finished tassels, showing long or short bugle beads.

The Lyndel Tassel

Requirements

Long beading needle

Nymo thread

Cotton tape woven, ¼ in (6 mm) wide, 3 in (7.5 cm) long

Upholstery gimp or braid of choice, ½ in (12 mm) wide,
2¾ in (7 cm) long

Fine cord of choice 10 in (25 cm)

Tassel top with a waist circumference 2¼–2½ in
(6–6.5 cm)

Beads

12 long bugle or 36 short bugle beads

Seed beads, first colour, 165

Seed beads, second colour, 143

Seed beads, black, 33

Feature dress or crystal beads, 11 large and 11 small

METHOD

❖ Mark the tape with dots ³⁄₁₆ in (½ cm) apart using a soft
lead pencil.

❖ Use a double thread approximately 24 in (60 cm) in length.

❖ Tie a knot at the end, and beginning ¾ in (2 cm) from the
end, bring the threaded needle from the back to the front of
the tape.

❖ Thread the beads using the dangle construction, shown in
diagram 5.

- ❖ Re-thread up through the bead marked * * on the diagram 5.

- ❖ Secure the threaded strand into the tape making sure that the beads lie straight.

- ❖ Move to the next dot and repeat the process to the end.

- ❖ Glue the fringe to the tassel waist, then glue on a covering braid, trim to fit.

- ❖ Knot the cord and thread through the tassel top using a wire loop.

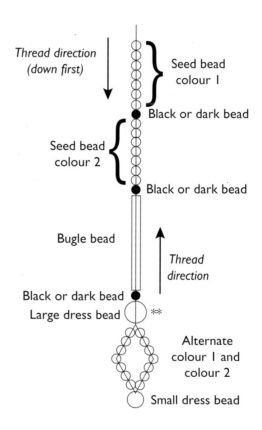

Diagram 5 – Lyndel Tassel Construction

Tassel Tops

These are available from most craft stores. For the purposes in this book two kinds were chosen. Wood turners will make them to specific requirements.

The diameter of the waist determines the number of strands of beads that fit. The closer the bead strands the fuller the tassel. The ruff, in particular, requires more strands of beads to give a much fuller tassel. Both purchased or hand-twisted cords are suitable for the tassel tops. Ribbons and rouleau can also be used — fine ribbons can be plaited while the wider widths lay flat.

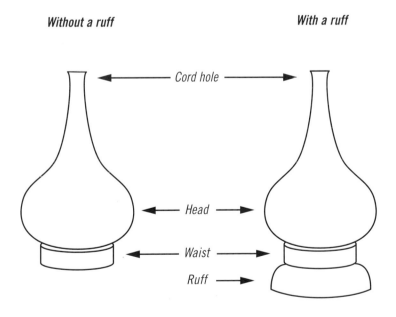

Without a ruff   **With a ruff**

Cord hole

Head

Waist

Ruff

Diagram 6 – Tassel Tops

Making a Tassel Brooch

Requirements

1 wooden button, ¾ in (2 cm) in diameter with two small holes drilled near the lower edge

1 very small wooden tassel top with ruff

Black tape or tape to match the tassel top colour, if painted

Covering braid or tape

Polyester-coated cotton quilting thread

Craft glue

Small amount of narrow decorative gimp or braid

1 long beading needle

1 brooch clip

Beads

10 g dark seed beads in the colour of your choice

12 silver or gold magatama beads (or small feature drops)

METHOD

❖ Lacquer, stain or paint the tassel top and the button.

❖ Thread the needle, with 24 in (60 cm) of thread when doubled.

❖ Knot the ends of the thread and sew to the edge of the tape with two tiny anchor stitches.

❖ Using the dangle method of construction, thread 21 dark seed beads, 1 magatama bead, then 3 more dark seed beads.

❖ Re-thread back through the eighth last bead, which will be a dark seed bead. This makes a loop at the end. Then, continue re-threading back up through the shaft all of the beads until you reach the tape. Check that the strand of beads is firm but not kinked.

❖ Stitch a tiny anchor stitch and then move on to start the next strand of beads leaving approximately a bead-width from the first strand.

❖ Continue until you have 12 or sufficient strands to fit around the waist of your tassel top.

❖ Glue the beaded fringe onto the waist of the tassel.

❖ Glue braid or tape on to cover the tape.

❖ Thread both cord ends through the holes of the button and the tassel top. Knot securely and pull the knot into the body of the tassel.

❖ If your button has a groove, on the double strand of cotton, thread sufficient beads to fit around the groove. Tie off the cotton tightly and glue the circle of beads into the groove as an added embellishment.

❖ Glue brooch base to the back of the button.

The Key Tassel

Key tassels are lovely to adorn both traditional and modern furniture, in fact, anywhere you have a key. This size tassel doubles for use on chair ties, lamps, doorknobs, as sun-catchers and on picture frames.

In colours that complement your décor, with stained, painted or gilded tops, these little decorating statements add a bit of glitz and glamour. Best of all, tassels can be used to trial patterns and colours that work well in combination. This becomes the start of a portfolio of ideas from which other ideas develop for use in larger projects. If a pattern works on a small scale, it will be easy to modify it for a lampshade fringe.

The Loré Tassels

The Christmas Tassel

Christmas tassels can be made in tiny showers of crystals or in bold red and green contrasting beads. A tiny Christmas tassel securing the wrapping on a parcel would be a lovely keepsake or a larger version could hang elegantly from a mistletoe wreath.

Santa Tassels

Two fancy tassel tops have been painted featuring Santa's head. There are three layers of fringing — one is rayon, the second is a long beaded fringe and the final, top layer is a short collar-like trim of beads.

Little Brooches

ANY PRETTY PAINTED SHAPE OR A BROOCH mounted on to a small wooden disc could be a suitable base for adding a small beaded fringe.

MAKING THE BROOCHES

❖ Simply, a ¾ in (2 cm) wide piece of folded bias fabric is ironed in half and marked into even sections. The distance apart depends on how closely you want the strands of beads to be placed and the sizes of the beads used.

❖ Keeping the length of the strands in proportion to the size of the disc, simply thread strands of beads in colours and patterns to suit your particular brooch face. Design your fringe with a longer central strand with a feature bead at the end. The other strands should begin to decrease on each side of the centre to form a gentle point. An uneven number of rows will work best. In the samples shown, no more than eleven strands have been used for the larger discs and two simple loops with a feature bead for the smaller ones.

❖ To finish off, glue the strip of fringing to the base of the disc following the shape of the curve. Cover with a neat ribbon or braid and add a brooch attachment.

Folk Art Brooches

A quaint collection of favourite brooches are embellished with small beaded fringes in coordinating colours.

Bookmarks

THIS METHOD IS SIMILAR TO THE INSTRUCTIONS for the scarf on page 92.

Here, small neat hems have been stitched at either end of the grosgrain ribbon. Then, a small fringe is made, stitching the strands of beads directly into the fabric. A feature at the end of the centre strand gives added interest.

The Ribbon
Flower Brooch

ATHER 2 YDS (1.82 M) OF SILK RIBBON AND
manipulate it into a flower shape, then mount
and secure it onto a small piece of buckram.
Add a few stamens or few wired beads. Using the same method
as those used for the disc brooches, add a decorative beaded
fringe.

Feature Tassels

IF YOU WORK THROUGH THE TASSELS IN THE ORDER suggested, you will find that your own preferences for designs will soon be evident. This will also open your own level of creativity and soon you will developing your own designs. It is recommended to begin with the Lyndel Tassel (see page 69). It has a simple pattern that is easy to remember and takes very little time to do. For your second attempt try the Colleen Tassel on page 86. This is an extension of the Lyndel Tassel. In this tassel, there is pattern variation, longer threads, a tassel top with a ruff and a greater number of strands. There are 27 strands that have been gathered to produce a fuller skirt of beads.

The Maureen Tassel is considered to be spectacular. A much longer tassel top with ruff forms the base of this tassel. Folk art and beads have been combined to achieve a good effect. Care must be taken when mixing two craft techniques so that the end product is viewed as a whole and not as two separate entities. The impact is derived from colour and bead choice and it is not more difficult than the previous tassel. Using the information provided from the pattern development section (see page 65), begin to use your own favourite combinations, substituting the colours of your choice to those shown. This larger tassel design would make very elaborate curtain tie-backs. The fringed beaded tassels give extra texture and combine dyed fringes with the beaded overlay. The possibilities are only limited by your imagination.

Two pairs of non-matching tassels, Lyn on the left, Faye on the right. Colours are similar but pattern variation in the beads has been done to give ideas for varying the designs. Two crafts combine — folk art tops and fringed, beaded skirts.

These have been made using various tassel tops that are readily available.

Some of them have ruffs others did not. Various kinds of yarn fringes have then been glued to the waist of the tassel tops. Next, a fringed skirt of beads in a simple pattern has been glued over the attached fringe, on the waist of the tassel.

Another feature layer is added on top of this if required. It is also glued to the waist part of the tassel. Finally, a decorative braid covers the workings and a twisted cord is threaded through the centre of the tassel.

To calculate your pattern, simply measure the waist circumference of the tassel top and divide it by the number of loops or strands that you want on your finished tassel. An odd number is more pleasing to the eye than an even number.

These are quick to make, use very few beads and the decorative impact is high.

The two large Santa tassels and all of the curtain tiebacks are simple ideas that could be varied to make very beautiful and original tassels. The popular half-doll tassels have been included for variety and interest.

Shown here are three styles of the feature half-dolls — The Modern (peach and black, right), The Flapper (amethyst and sage, centre) and The Marie-Antoinette (lime and pink, left) Tassels. They show some successful bead and colour pattern variations.

The Colleen Tassel

Requirements

1 tassel top with ruff

Cotton thread

Long beading needle

Craft glue

White paint

Small paint brush

Soft lead pencil

Woven cotton tape, ¼ in (6 mm) wide, 5½ in (14 cm) long

Braid or gimp, ½ in (12 mm) wide, 4 in (10 cm) long

Decorative gimp or braid, 4 in (10 cm) long

Fine pink and white cord, 10 in (25 cm) long

416 pink seed beads

650 white seed beads

156 small dress beads

26 large dress beads

78 short white bugle beads

METHOD

❖ Paint the tassel top white. Cut the braid tape slightly larger than given.

❖ Mark the tape with a dot at ³⁄₁₆ in (4 mm) intervals using a soft lead pencil.

❖ Complete 27 strands of the pattern.

❖ Run a small gathering thread along the length of the tape

and pull up evenly to fit the waist of the tassel top. Then, glue it to the waist.

❖ Cover the tape with the braid.

❖ Thread the fine pink and white cord through the tassel top and glue the ends into tassel top.

The Colleen Tassel

The Colleen Tassel is an extension of the Lyndel tassel with the following variation — each strand of the pattern is longer, more strands are required and the tassel top is different. In this sample the tassel top with a ruff consists of 27 strands in the fringing. These have been gathered to fit the waist above the ruff and so produce a fuller skirt of beads.

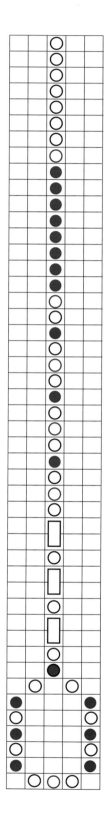

● Small pink seed bead
○ Small pink dress bead
○ White seed bead
▢ Short white bugle bead
● Large pink dress bead

**Diagram 7 –
The Colleen Tassel**

*Thread cord through tassel
top and glue it into place.*

The Maureen Tassel

Requirements

1 tassel top with ruff, waist diameter 4½ in (11 cm) (decorated if desired)

Cotton thread

Long beading needle

Craft glue

Soft lead pencil

Woven cotton tape ¼ in (6 mm) wide, 4½ in (11.5 cm) long

Braid or gimp ½ in (12 mm) wide, 4½ in (11.5 cm) long

Amethyst, pink and gold twisted cord, desired length for hanging

87 pink/mauve bugle beads

116 white seed beads

58 black seed beads

406 gold seed beads

116 amethyst seed beads

364 small dark mauve Delica seed beads

27 dark amethyst crystals

27 small amethyst dress beads

METHOD

❖ Decorate the tassel top as desired. Cut the cotton tape slightly longer than given to cover the waist of your tassel. The remainder can be trimmed.

❖ Mark the tape with dots at 3⁄16 in (4 mm) intervals using the soft lead pencil.

The Maureen Tassel has a
much longer tassel top
complete with a ruff. Folk
art and beads have been
combined to achieve this
distinction. This pattern
also makes a lovely tie-back
for curtains.

- ❖ Complete 27 strands of the pattern.

- ❖ Fit and glue the fringe to the tassel waist.

- ❖ Cover the tape with braid or gimp, glue it on and trim to fit.

- ❖ Thread the twisted cord through the tassel top and glue onto the base of the tassel top.

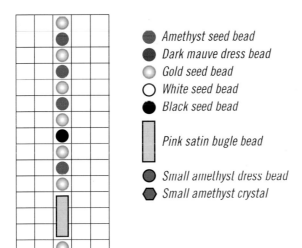

- ● Amethyst seed bead
- ● Dark mauve dress bead
- ○ Gold seed bead
- ○ White seed bead
- ● Black seed bead

▌ Pink satin bugle bead

- ● Small amethyst dress bead
- ⬡ Small amethyst crystal

Diagram 8 – The Maureen Tassel

A Beaded Scarf

A SCARF IS ALWAYS A DELIGHTFUL ACCESSORY AND this particular style is easily adaptable between work attire and an evening function. Here, fine dress jet bugles and navy iridescent seed beads are combined to give added sparkle.

The fabric has been lined and then a fringe has been stitched onto the edges of the length of fabric. Small beads or light-weight beads are most suitable for this purpose.

Requirements

Black cotton or black Nymo thread

Beading needle

6½ in (16 cm) fabric (wool or polyester crepe would be suitable)

6½ in (16 cm) lining (a light polyester would be suitable)

50g navy iridescent seed beads

50g short black dress bugles

Note Light-weight dress bugles and small seed beads must be used to ensure that the scarf is easy to wear.

METHOD

❖ Lay the two pieces of fabric, right sides together and hand or machine-stitch the outside edges together, leaving a small section in the side seam to facilitate turning.

❖ Steam press, turn to the right side and hand-stitch the opened section closed.

❖ Mark the top edge of the scarf into equal ¼ in (6 mm) sections. The central position is the starting point, so sew a small coloured stitch above this dot.

❖ Beginning at the centre, follow the sequence to the outer edge — one seed bead, one bugle bead, one seed bead. Then, with 3 or 5 seed beads, form a loop at the end of each strand.

❖ Check that the strand is firm but not kinked and sew a small stay-stitch. Move to the next dot and decrease by one seed bead and one bugle bead on each strand until all the rows are completed.

❖ Repeat this pattern on the other side of the centre.

❖ Work the bottom edge in the same way.

❖ There is no covering braid on the scarf, so neat stitching is most important. Each strand is sewn individually. Take care that the advance thread, the thread in the needle, comes from the wrong side of the scarf to the right and is hidden in the edge of the fabric before commencing the next strand.

❖ Wear your lovely scarf with pride!

Evening Bags

This evening bag, centre, is decorated with a panel of black, amethyst and silver beads and the fringe would work equally well applied to the bottom of a straight-edged purchased evening bag or perhaps, teamed with a scarf. Other photographs show variations.

Beaded Comb

Requirements

1 plastic hair comb. Clear combs work well with all hair
colours

Cotton or Nymo thread

Beading needle

Strong craft glue

Small piece of woven cotton tape slightly longer than the
length of the top rim of the comb so that the edges can
be folded over

Small piece of braid to match the beads slightly longer
than the length of the top rim of the comb so that the
edges can be folded over

20g iridescent seed beads

20g short twisted bugle beads

Feature bead or crystal drop for the centre strand

Soft lead pencil

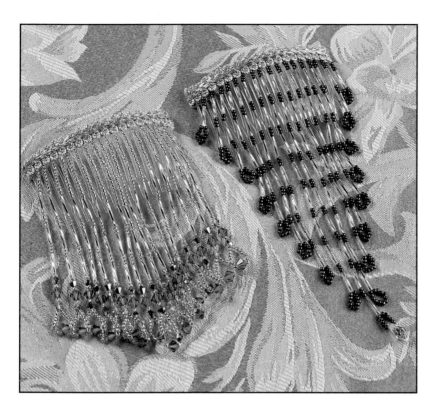

METHOD

❖ Mark the tape with a dot into ³⁄₁₆ in (4 mm) sections using a soft lead pencil.

❖ Stitch a small stay-stitch with contrasting-coloured thread to mark the centre strand. This is the longest strand and can have a feature crystal or drop.

❖ Using about a 1 yd (approximately 1 m) of the cotton or Nymo thread, doubled in the needle, stay-stitch the thread into the centre mark and begin the pattern.

❖ Decrease by one bugle (or two seed beads) on each strand to the side edge of the comb.

❖ Repeat from the other side of the centre strand.

❖ Glue the fringe to the comb and then glue the braid over the top of it.

Note that the small bugle beads sit better with a small seed bead on either side.

Shelves

BEADED SHELVES LOOK BEST IN STRONG COLOURS with a reasonable number of gold/silver and cut beads in the pattern. The light that reflects from the beads is either daylight or reflected night light. Under these circumstances the sparkle is from the surface light and is dependent on bead choice and placement. The shelf could be lit from underneath and would be worth the expense if the beads in the project had either a strong sentimental or historic value.

The shelves are secured using two framing cord holders. The hooks are placed just above the edge of the shelf. Another method is to use double-sided tape, but the location would be permanent and no heavy objects would be able to be displayed.

When measuring the working tape and the finishing braid, a good idea is to add a small extra amount to wrap behind the edge of the shelf for a neat finish.

Shelves work very well in corners and for this, a circle of an appropriate radius would have to be cut in four sections. This would give four shelves to bead.

Santa Shelf Project

Requirements

1 semi-circle of timber for the shelf. One circle of timber with a radius of 2⅜ in (6 cm) when cut, will give two semicircular shelves with a curved edge of 8¾ in (22 cm)

2 pieces of braid 9¼ in (23 cm) for edge decoration

Beading needle

Thread

Tape or folded bias in colour to match the braid, 9¼ in (23 cm)

Craft glue

642 gold seed beads

41 large red dress beads

150 small red dress beads

96 black seed beads

96 gold twisted bugle beads, ½ in (12 mm)

48 olive medium crystals

48 small, clear crystals

3 clear drop crystals or feature daggers

METHOD

❖ Paint, lacquer or gild the shelf.

❖ Make the beaded fringe according to one of the combinations shown in diagram 10.

❖ Glue onto the curved edge of the shelf.

❖ Cover the edge with decorative braids. If using two, glue the gold on first.

Note There are three pattern repeats and the spacing is ³⁄₁₆ in (5 mm) between the strands. Any appropriate drop can act as the feature at the end of the centre strand of each pattern.

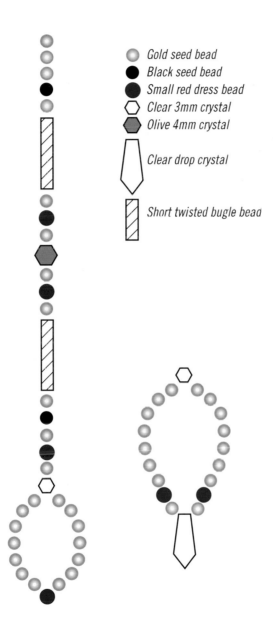

Gold seed bead
Black seed bead
Small red dress bead
Clear 3mm crystal
Olive 4mm crystal

Clear drop crystal

Short twisted bugle bead

Diagram 10 - The Santa Shelf

The Nina Shelf

Requirements

1 semi-circle of timber for the shelf (One circle of timber with a radius of 4 in (10 cm), when cut, gives two semi-circular shelves with a curved edge measuring 13 in (33 cm).)

1 piece of braid, 14 in (35.5cm) long and wide enough to cover the edge as a trim

Beading needle

Thread

Tape or folded bias to match the braid, 14 in (35.5 cm)

Craft glue

20 g gold seed beads

20 g aqua seed beads

200 medium jade crystals

70 medium dark aqua crystals

200 medium black AB round beads

3 feature beads or tear drops for the centre of each panel

300 aqua/jade mix of short bugle beads

METHOD

❖ Paint, lacquer or gild the shelf.

❖ Make the beaded fringe according to diagram 11. There are three pattern repeats. Strand one is shown. It has five beads in the top section (that is, one gold, one aqua, one gold, one aqua, one gold). Simply increase by two beads in this section of the pattern until you have 25 beads for the middle strand. Then decrease by two beads until you are back to the five beads in the top section.

❖ Glue the finished fringing onto the edge of the shelf and then cover the edge with a decorative braid.

Note The shelf shown here uses two braids to finish the edge. When using two braids, the narrower of the two is glued on first.

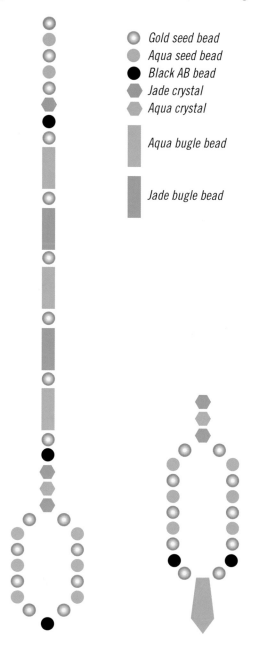

Gold seed bead
Aqua seed bead
Black AB bead
Jade crystal
Aqua crystal

Aqua bugle bead

Jade bugle bead

Diagram 11 –
The Nina Shelf

Dyeing Fringes

T he colour range in fringing is quite extensive, but for those projects when a perfect match to the fabric or when mixed colours within one fringe is required, it is simple to dye your own.

White is the best colour base but some pale creams are also very effective.

The various fibres, such as silk, cotton and rayon, respond differently to the dye medium, so it is desirable to experiment on small samples of the fringe first to determine the results.

The cut ends of fringes tend to unravel and over time develop a fluffy look, but looped fringes hang and wear well. However, the finished texture is very much a matter of personal choice.

Requirements

Maddies craft dye (three primary colours — yellow, red and blue)

Follow the directions on the chart located on the packaging bearing in mind that different threads will respond differently to the dyes. Experimentation on small pieces of fringing is vital. Dyes can be 'fixed' with the addition of salt when mixing the dye. Always use rubber gloves.

Two-Colour Fringe

METHOD

❖ Place the prepared dyes in shallow plastic dishes (rectangular take-away dishes are suitable).

❖ Fold the length of fringing required in half and roll up into a tight cylinder starting at the two cut ends.

❖ Dip one end into the prepared dye, then gently squeeze to remove any excess.

❖ Dip the other end into the second colour — gently squeeze to remove any excess.

❖ Twist the length of fringing so that the two colours will blend.

❖ Dry in a gentle breeze away from the sun.

❖ Dye any braid to match while you have the desired mix.

Note All the projects using dyed fringes in this book have been made using cold water dyes. If, however, you live in a humid climate, there is a possibility that the dye could run into fabric such as a curtain fold. It is important to set the cold water dyes with added salt. Otherwise — use water dyes which are guaranteed not to run.

The Marion Shade

A straight-edge empire lampshade has twelve patterns of olive green, amethyst, gold and black. This would be an excellent first project.

The Marion Lamp

After choosing a base with sufficient stem or candle height to take a fringe measuring 5–5½ in (12.5–14 cm) at the longest strand. Work out your own colours simply by changing the most dominant colour in the pattern.

Requirements

10 in (25 cm) straight empire shade

½ yd (50 cm) of fabric for covering

½ yd (50 cm) of lining fabric

1 yd (1 m) of tape for mounting the strands of beads

1 yd (1 m) of braid for covering the finished length of beaded fringing

Nymo or Coates polyester coated cotton quilting thread

2 No. 2C CrownFox needles

800 gold seed beads

160 black seed beads

800 amethyst seed beads

600 small olive dress or 600 crystals for extra sparkle

200 gold 1 in (2.5 cm) bugle beads

300 large olive dress

12 feature glass or crystal drops

Detail of the Marion Shade

METHOD

❖ The pattern shaping occurs in the top section of gold beads.
The rest of the pattern is constant except for the middle
strand of each pattern that has a feature at the end. Each
strand changes by only two seed beads, that is increases up
to the centre strand, decreases to the end of the pattern.

❖ Make your beaded fringe allowing two patterns per section.
Follow the method as shown in the Lyndel Tassel. Note that
the pattern shaping changes from three gold seed beads up

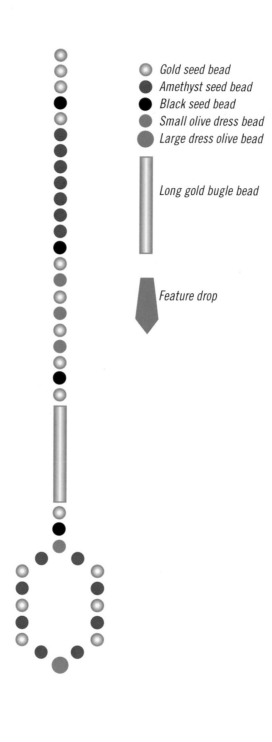

Gold seed bead
Amethyst seed bead
Black seed bead
Small olive dress bead
Large dress olive bead

Long gold bugle bead

Feature drop

Diagram 12 —
The Marion Shade

to fifteen gold seed beads for the centre strand. The pattern is then reduced by two beads in each row until you have repeated the first three gold seed beads row. This forms a gentle chevron pattern.

❖ When you have completed 12 patterns, run a small gathering thread across your beaded tape to give gentle ease when fitting. Use glue or stitch to the shade edge and carefully fit the fringe using spring pegs to secure. Move the pegs to a new space as you go so they do not attach to the edge.

❖ Allow to dry and then glue or stitch on the covering braid. You may need a double braid to cover the workings on for further embellishment. View in situ on the base fitting with a lit glove for best effect.

Note The bead quantities are best purchased in bulk as the amounts given are most economical for the project.

Ready covered frames are suitable. Gently remove the edge embellishment and you may be able to reuse it after applying your beaded fringing. Covered frames can be ordered with your own fabric choice. Refer to the list of suppliers on page 116.

Gift Ideas

CHRISTMAS THEMES

How lovely it is to receive a handmade gift! It is especially wonderful if that gift has been made in your favourite colours or personalised with your initials.

The gifts shown throughout this book are such tributes. Each is very simple and elegant and made from quality materials that will not date.

Christmas colour combinations can be from deep purple-red and deep forest green to bright Christmas red and green. White, gold and silver make up the filler beads. The creative possibilities are endless.

The Christmas Lamp

The Christmas Lamp on a shelf of timber and a large ornamental stag is the main the feature of the base. The candle of the lamp is made from a small branch that as been drilled through the centre to contain the electrical cord. A traditional red silk shade has been fringed with gold and silver beads. The Christmas tree echoes the festive colours. Lit by the Christmas Lamp are stockings, bookmarks and parcel tassels.

Glossary

AB Beads — This refers to the iridescent finish on the surface of the bead. It gives the face of the bead extra shine in colours of purple, green and blue.

Buckram — Coarse cloth stiffened with sizing.

Delica — Brand of seed beads available in a wide colour range.

Gimp — The preferred edge finish for beaded lampshades. This is cotton yarn, overspun for a smooth finish with rayon or similar thread.

Loop — The section at the end of a strand of beads needed to facilitate a turn.

Junction bead — Usually marked on the pattern or chart with one or two asterisks. This is the bead through which the double thread passes twice — once on the downward part of the loop and then on the return section of the loop.

Magatama bead — This is a small oval bead which tapers at the top. A seed bead sits snugly either side and is useful for the ends of loops.

Panel or section — The distance between two struts on the frame of the shade.

Pattern — A design made using several stands of beads.

Strand — A length of beads on a double strand of thread.

Tape — Woven cotton tape or folded bias strips onto which the strands of the beads are secured.

Verdigris — Green film on copper.

Suppliers

Commissions, classes and tassel tops
Beth Bulluss
22 Gemini Avenue
ELERMORE VALE NSW 2287
Australia
Ph: (02) 4951 6106
email: beadedlamps@kooee.com.au

Fringing, beads, braid
Photios Bros
66 Druitt Street
SYDNEY NSW 2000
Australia
Ph: (02) 9267 1428

Shades
Covered in fabric of your choice and ready to bead:
Barbara Maloney
Creative Lampshades
6 Jefferson Street
ADAMSTOWN NSW 2289
Australia
Ph: (02) 4952 6401

Shade frames
Available from selected craft stores nationally

Beads
The Australian Bead Company
PO Box 243
HURSTVILLE NSW 1481
Australia
Ph: (02) 9546 4544

OLAF Beadwork
PO Box 558
NOARLUNGA CENTRE SA 5164
Australia
Ph: (08) 8326 0833
Fax: (08) 8326 2411

Maria George Beads
179 Flinders Lane
MELBOURNE VIC 3000
Australia
Ph: (03) 9650 1151
Fax: (03) 9650 5313

Dyes
Maddies Corner Cottage
80 Pembroke Road
MOOROOLBARK VIC 3138
Australia
Ph/Fax: (03) 9728 5628

Beads/braid/needles and thread
Anlaby Designs
157 Swan Street
MORPETH NSW 2321
Australia
‚ 8234

Shipwreck Beads
2500 Mottman Road SW
OLYMPIA WA 98512
United States of America
www.shipwreck-beads.com

Beads Galore
2123S. Priest, Suite 201
TEMPE AZ 85282
United States of America

Beadworks
126 West 3rd Ave
2nd Floor
VANCOUVER BC V5YIE9
Canada
www.beadworkswholesale.com

Lighting
Rovert Lighting
4 Bronte Road
BROADMEADOW NSW 2241
Ph: (02) 4952 5600

Acknowledgements

Special thanks to my family and friends for their support.

Thank you for your valued contributions to:

Barbara Maloney for the shade coverings

Dudley Keevers for woodturning and lamp base modifications

Lore Barratt for the folk art and painted finishes

Marion Smith for the silk flowers

Lyndel Coleman for assistance with word processing and diagrams

Julieanne Tilse for assistance with diagrams

Clients who have allowed me to use their lampshades and bases in some of the photographs are Lee Thomas, Margaret McMellon, Carol Whiteside, Joy Brown, Marie Messmer, Robin Rietdijk and Marion Smith.

Beth Bulluss

(photo courtesy Hunter Lifestyle Magazine)